Saltwater Secrets

CAMBRIDGE PUBL
W9-AFU-737

FAMILIES of the Deep Blue Sea

AMIGOS SCHOOL
LIBRARY
Cambridge, MA 02139

by **Kenneth Mallory** and the

 New England Aquarium

illustrated by
Marshall Peck III

ini **Charlesbridge**

To Stars, Stripes, and Forever, an extended family of North Atlantic right whales who may mean the difference between species survival or extinction — KM

For Beth — MP III

Text copyright © 1995 by Charlesbridge Publishing
Illustrations copyright © 1995 by Marshall Peck III
All rights reserved, including the right of
reproduction in whole or in part in any form.

Published by
Charlesbridge Publishing
85 Main Street, Watertown, MA 02172-4411
(617) 926-0329

Printed in Hong Kong
(sc) 10 9 8 7 6 5 4 3 2
(hc) 10 9 8 7 6 5 4 3 2 1

Printed on Recycled Paper.

Library of Congress Cataloging-in-Publication Data
Mallory, Kenneth.
    Families of the deep blue sea / by Kenneth Mallory;
illustrated by Marshall Peck III.
        p.   cm. — (Saltwater secrets)
    ISBN 0-88106-887-X (library reinforced)
    ISBN 0-88106-886-1 (hardcover)
    ISBN 0-88106-885-3 (softcover)
    1. Marine fauna—Infancy—Juvenile literature. 2. Parental
behavior in animals. [1. Marine animals—Infancy. 2. Parental
behavior in animals.] I. Peck, Marshall H. II. Title. III. Series.
QL122.2.M36   1995
591.3'9'09162 — dc20   95-7039
                                          CIP
                                          AC

Do you know how saltwater families live? What would it be like to grow up with a tail and fins? We expect to see fish living in water, but what about mammals like polar bears, walruses, and whales, or birds such as penguins, or reptiles like sea turtles? They spend most of their lives in the water, too.

How would it feel to be born, to grow, to play and explore the way these ocean-dwelling animals do? Here's your chance to find out. Jump in and learn the saltwater secrets of growing up in the sea!

Imagine that you are a walrus pup. Your mother has long, pointed tusks that she uses to protect you from hungry killer whales and stray polar bears. You can look forward to having your own 3-foot-long tusks when you are a 2,000 pound grown-up walrus!

To grow that big, you need to find food by feeling around on the muddy ocean bottom with the 450 bristly hairs on your cheek pads. When you find clams and mussels, you hold them between your lips and suck them out of their shells.

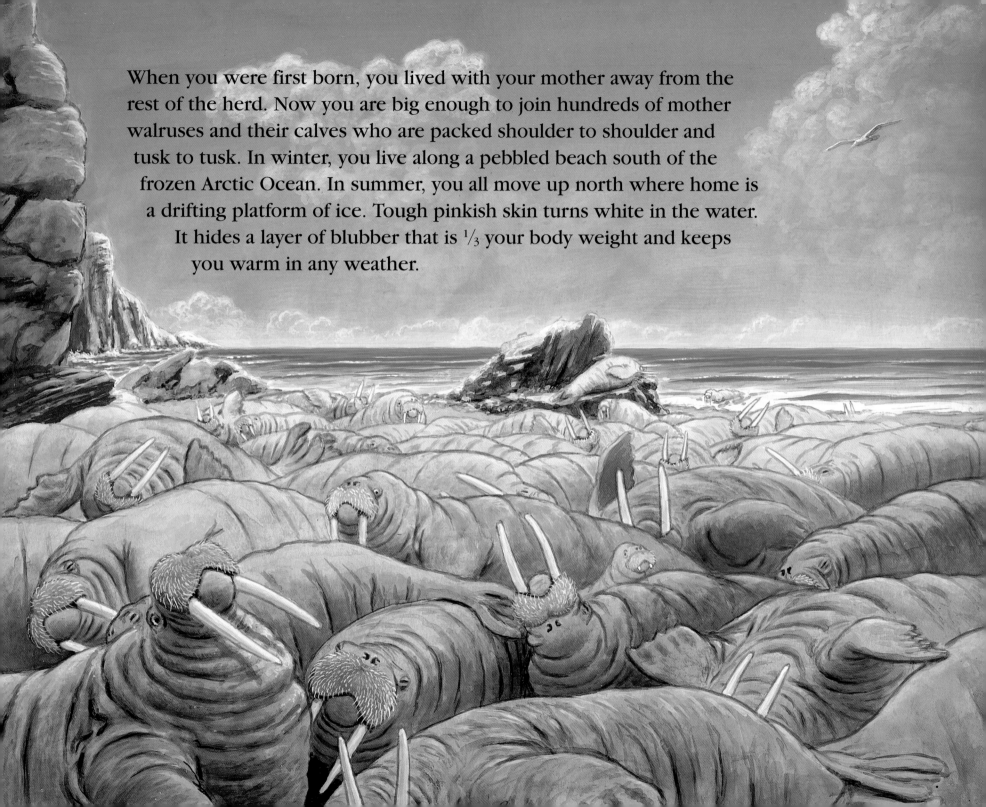

When you were first born, you lived with your mother away from the rest of the herd. Now you are big enough to join hundreds of mother walruses and their calves who are packed shoulder to shoulder and tusk to tusk. In winter, you live along a pebbled beach south of the frozen Arctic Ocean. In summer, you all move up north where home is a drifting platform of ice. Tough pinkish skin turns white in the water. It hides a layer of blubber that is $\frac{1}{3}$ your body weight and keeps you warm in any weather.

Pretend you are growing up in a
crocodile family. Your life begins in a
watertight egg. All the food you need is in
the yolk and egg white. When it's time to hatch,
you use a special hard ridge on the end of your long
toothy snout to help you to break out of the eggshell.

Your mother comes running when she hears you chirping. There are no animals big enough or tough enough to bother her. As soon as you are out in the big world of the seashore and nearby freshwater swamps, you begin to hunt for fish, insects, and small shellfish. When dangerous predators come hunting for crocodile snacks in your neighborhood, you swim for the safety of your mom's back.

Imagine growing up in an emperor penguin family somewhere near the South Pole.

You are born in a pear-shaped egg. Your father holds your egg on his feet, pressed against his warm belly and covered by a flap of skin that is like a protective overcoat.

Two months later, during a day when the sun never rises, you come out of your shell into a winter sixty-degrees-below-zero.

Your parents take turns searching for fish to eat and to feed you. You eat all your dinner so you will grow to be nearly 100 pounds like your mom and dad. By the beginning of the Antarctic summer, you are ready to make the long march to the edge of the sea ice. You molt your soft, brown, baby feathers and grow a new set of feathers that are waterproof. Now you are ready to learn the joys of flying underwater to chase after squid and fish.

Can you imagine what it's like to be a giant octopus? You start your life in an egg the size of a grain of rice. Together with seventy thousand brothers and sisters, you dangle in your eggshells from the roof of an underwater cave like a string of holiday decorations. Your mother wraps you up in her protective tentacles and keeps you clean by pumping water over you, day and night. If any dangerous fish swim by, she changes her color to red and attacks, chasing them away. She is exhausted from tending her many eggs and dies by the time you are ready to hatch. Fortunately, as an octopus baby, you can take care of yourself.

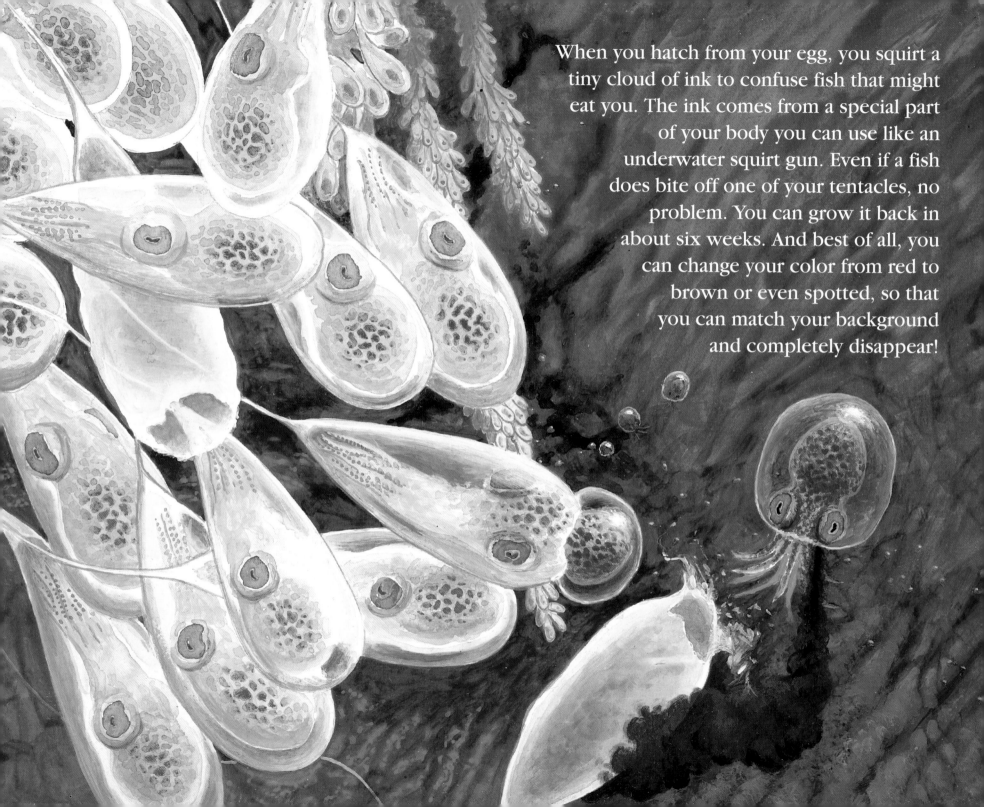

When you hatch from your egg, you squirt a tiny cloud of ink to confuse fish that might eat you. The ink comes from a special part of your body you can use like an underwater squirt gun. Even if a fish does bite off one of your tentacles, no problem. You can grow it back in about six weeks. And best of all, you can change your color from red to brown or even spotted, so that you can match your background and completely disappear!

Picture yourself as a sea otter pup. When you are born in the cold waters of the North Pacific Ocean, your mother dries your fur until it is soft and fluffy. Because, like all otters, you don't have a thick, insulating layer of fat, you depend on clean, dry fur to hold in your body heat. Your mother feeds you her warm milk while you are riding on her belly. In less than a year, you will be almost as big as she is.

During your first year, your mother shows you how to use your belly as a lunch table. You lie on your back and crack open clams with a stone. You also learn to dive down 100 feet deep to hunt for snails, crabs, and clams to eat. But there is plenty of time to play hide-and-seek among the floating forests of kelp seaweeds that are part of your ocean classroom.

Let's pretend you are a harbor seal pup. Your mother looks like a big wet dog. Born on a beach or a wave-splashed rock, you take underwater rides holding onto your mother's blubbery neck. Your food is milk from the nipples hidden under fur along her belly.

When you are a few months old, you follow your mother to hunt
shrimp and fish. You find your food by swimming on your
back so you can see the ocean bottom more easily.
When you become separated from your mother,
you can find her by her special smell. Rubbing
whiskers with her is your way to say, "Hello."

Imagine growing up in a family of dolphins. Born underwater, tail-first, you stay with your mother for the first few years of your life. Clicks and whistles are your ways of talking.

A day-care center for baby dolphins? Yes, if you are a baby dolphin, your mother doesn't need to keep an eye on you all the time. When she's busy with your big sister, other mothers will baby-sit for you.

They swim around you and the other babies to keep watch. When you grow older, you will join other young dolphins in groups to play and learn to hunt.

Picture yourself in a cardinal fish family. Your parents could hide your egg under a rock or in a patch of seaweed, but they have a safer way to protect you. Your dad is a mouth brooder. He keeps eggs safe by holding them in his mouth. Together with dozens of brothers and sisters, you make your father's mouth puff out like a partly inflated balloon.

When you hatch inside his mouth, you swim out into the wet
world although you are no bigger than a speck. When hunting
fish swim by, you dart back into the safety of his mouth.
Sometimes though, hiding in your
father's mouth can be dangerous.
He might forget that you are there
and swallow some food, and you
right along with it!

Let's pretend you are a polar bear cub. You are born a helpless, little ball of skin barely covered with thin, short hair, and not much bigger than a newborn kitten. Your eyes stay tightly closed for the first few months of your life. You snuggle on your mother's chest, warmed by her hot breath and fat-rich milk.

When you are four months old, your family leaves the protection of your snow cave and heads for the open ocean, miles away. Huge, floating platforms of ice will now become your home. But, before you can float off on the ice, you need to learn how to swim. Your front feet are like large paddles, perfect for swimming. They have fur on the bottom so that you do not slip on the wet ice. Soon you are ready to learn to hunt the ringed seal that will become one of your favorite foods.

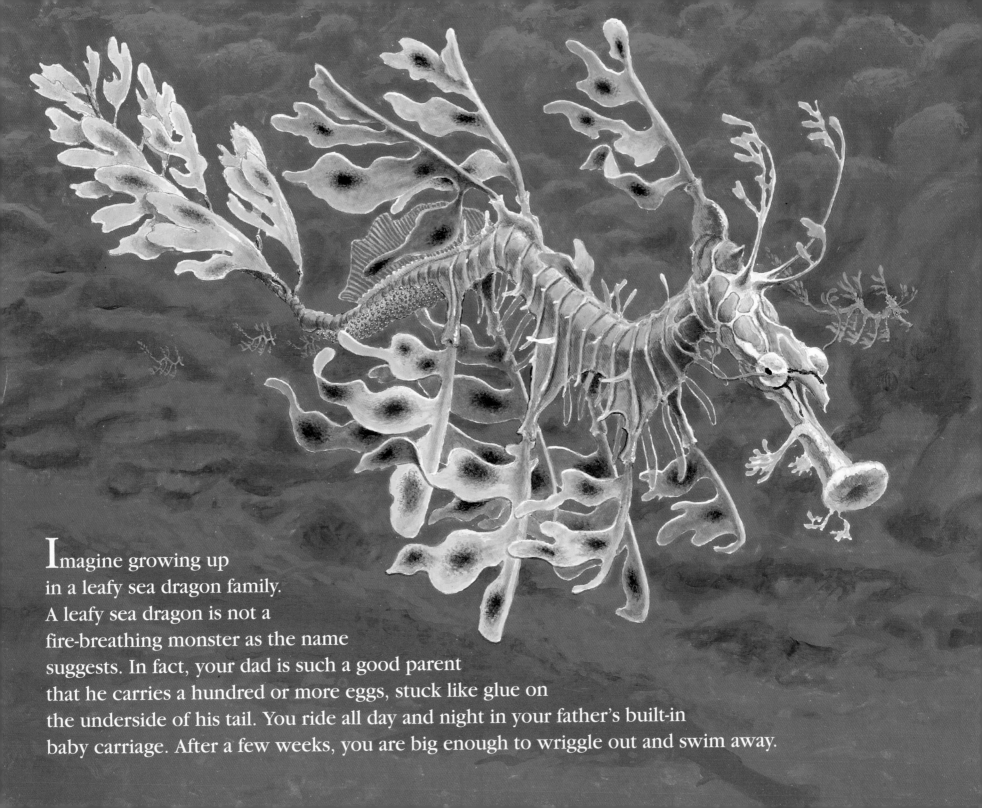

Imagine growing up
in a leafy sea dragon family.
A leafy sea dragon is not a
fire-breathing monster as the name
suggests. In fact, your dad is such a good parent
that he carries a hundred or more eggs, stuck like glue on
the underside of his tail. You ride all day and night in your father's built-in
baby carriage. After a few weeks, you are big enough to wriggle out and swim away.

Like your relative, the sea horse, you swim by flapping your fins or by lurching your body back and forth like a rocking horse. If a hungry fish swims up, will you swim away as fast as a race horse? No, sea dragons are very slow swimmers. You rely on your leafy body to blend in so well with the seaweed of your underwater home that the fish cannot see you. Hiding in the weeds, you can slurp up the plankton soup of tiny plants and animals into your trumpetlike mouth.

Imagine being a North Atlantic right whale calf. When you are born, you have patches of gray-and-white callused skin called callosities (kal-loss-it-tees) and you are over fifteen feet long! Your patches are as unique as a fingerprint and probably help your mother tell you apart from other right whale calves. Because whales are mammals, you breathe with lungs, not with gills like a fish.

To get food from your mother, you have to hold your breath while she squirts milk into your mouth.

After gaining 2,000 pounds in your first month, you are ready to migrate from the warm waters off the coast of Florida to the cooler waters off the coast of Maine and Canada.

On the way north, your mom shows you how to use the bristly
baleen combs inside your mouth to strain swarms of tiny plants from the water.
If a fishing boat goes by, your mom slaps her tail on the water to call you closer. Since only 300
North Atlantic right whales are still alive today, your mother's protection might
mean the difference between extinction and survival for your species.

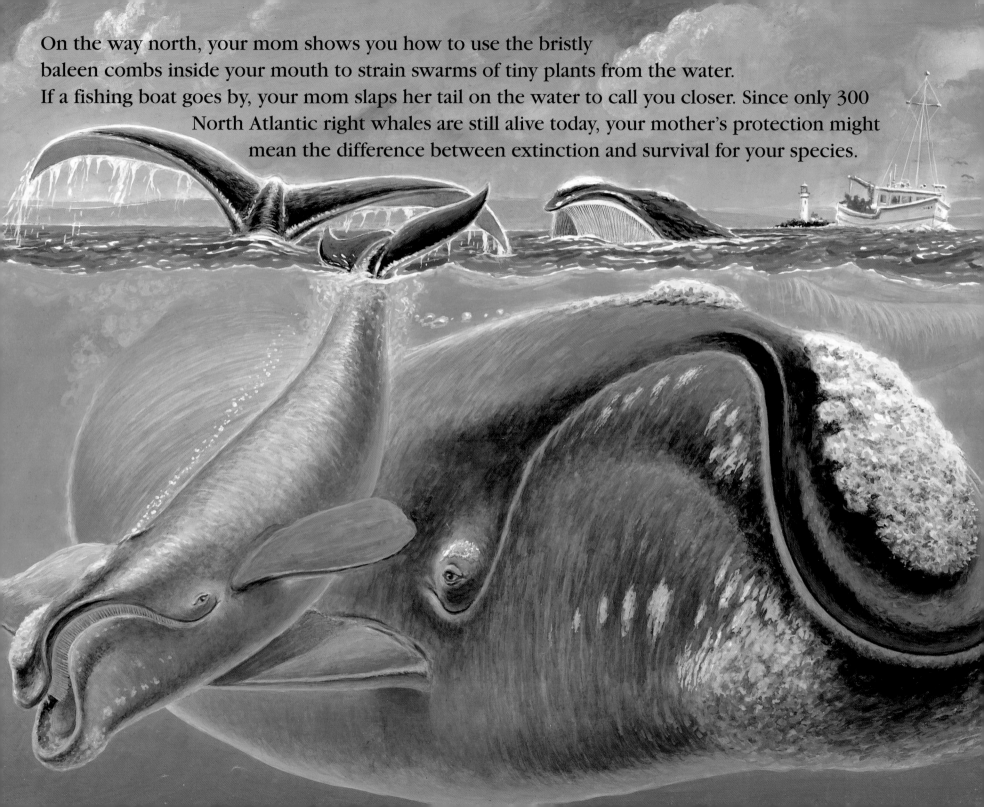

Picture yourself as a member of the largest sea turtle family, the leatherback sea turtles. You will grow up to be over six feet long and weigh a ton.

Even though your father and mother are giants, they can't wait around for you to hatch. You and your brothers and sisters climb out of your sandy nest on a moonlit night and run for the ocean. If you are lucky enough to escape the birds, crabs, and raccoons looking for an easy meal, you still have to survive the sharks and other hungry fishes hunting in the shallows of the sea.

When you grow up, you eat such tasty treats as sea nettles and other sea jellies. Without a care, you slurp up their stinging tentacles like spaghetti. Swimming thousands of miles across the ocean each year, you keep your journey a mystery until you are ready to bury eggs of your own, often on the same beach where you were born.

Imagine being a young coral catfish. Your parents are not around to protect you.

There are many bigger fish that would like to eat you, so you learn to swim so close to your brothers and sisters that you all look like one big fish! Big fishes stay away because they are afraid you might eat them!

Of course, it's not always possible to have brothers and sisters close by when danger threatens. But don't worry, you can use the poison spines on your back and sides to defend yourself against your enemies. Most fish stay away while you use your long whiskers to feel around for food. They know that your yellow-and-black stripes mean danger just like the stripes of a wasp or bee.

Let's pretend you are a sand tiger shark. You grow inside your mother just like a mammal baby. As you grow, you get so hungry that you eat your smaller brothers and sisters. By the time you are ready to be born, you are fat enough to survive on your own without anyone to take care of you.

For a shark pup, survival means hiding from the bigger hunters of the sea. You have to watch out every minute or a big fish like a grouper will pounce on you before you can grow big enough to fight back. Your only chance is to swim away fast.

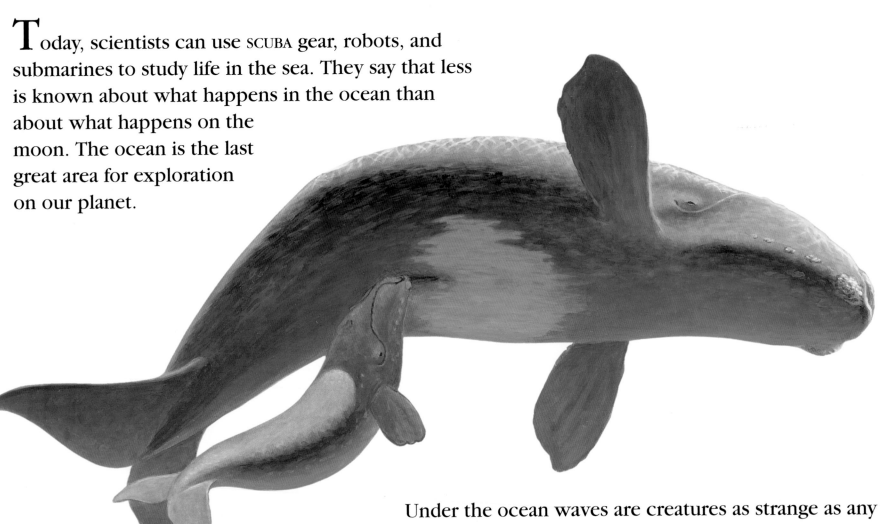

Today, scientists can use SCUBA gear, robots, and submarines to study life in the sea. They say that less is known about what happens in the ocean than about what happens on the moon. The ocean is the last great area for exploration on our planet.

Under the ocean waves are creatures as strange as any that we could imagine. They have adapted to live under every condition, in every depth, and in amazing families. These families have been around for thousands of years in an endless chain of parents and children. But, saltwater animals can only thrive if the ocean they live in and the nurseries they depend on remain protected and pollution free. And that depends on the wisdom and care of another family of mammals — you and me.